Victorian Embroidery Patterns:

Elegant
Floral Borders

edited by Moira Allen

A Publication of
Victorian
Voices.net

Books available from VictorianVoices.net:

Victorian Embroidery Patterns: Fabulous Florals Vol. 1
Victorian Embroidery Patterns: Fabulous Florals Vol. 2
Victorian Embroidery Patterns: Elegant Floral Borders
Victorian Embroidery Patterns: Alphabets & Initials

Needle-Crafts from a Victorian Workbasket

A Victorian Christmas Treasury I & II

Time for Tea: Victorian Tea-Time Treats & Decadent Desserts

The Laugh-Out-Loud Victorian Poetry Collection
(Six slim volumes of wickedly funny Victorian verse)

Bits About Animals: A Treasury of Victorian Animal Anecdotes

English as She Is Taught

Graveyard Humor: Quaint and Curious Inscriptions & Epitaphs

Visit VictorianVoices.net/bookstore/books.shtml for details

Copyright © 2021 Moira Allen
Published by Moira Allen via Kindle Direct Publishing
ISBN: 9798539826277

Introduction

Welcome to the first volume in the *Victorian Embroidery Patterns* series: *Elegant Floral Borders*. This collection brings you 374 beautiful patterns for borders, edges, and continuous patterns (often used as "insertions" in Victorian days). You'll find both realistic and abstract flower designs, as well as designs for leaves and plants.

In Victorian times, these patterns would have been used to ornament skirts and blouses, handkerchiefs, children's garments, household décor such as curtains and tablecloths, pillows and chair covers, and more. "Outline" patterns might be worked in chain stitch, or used for the application of braid to clothing or other items (such as slippers!). We've included patterns worked on net and lace as inspiration for today's needlework applications.

These patterns come from a host of the best women's and family magazines of the Victorian era, including *Godey's Lady's Book, Peterson's Magazine, Ingalls' Home Magazine, The Ladies' Home Journal, The Girl's Own Paper (UK), Cassell's Family Magazine (UK), Demorest,* and many others. Please note that any captions or instructions are part of the original image.

Since "scale" was rarely relevant in the original illustrations (which might be printed at any size according to how much space was on the page), these patterns cannot be said to be "in scale." Rather, they can be enlarged or reduced as needed, according to the project at hand. They are printed on one side of the page for ease of use – but to make life even easier, we've set up a free download of all the patterns in this book, at their full original sizes. Most of these patterns are available at 600 dpi, making them suitable for nearly any project! Please see the end of the book for the download link.

These and hundreds of other Victorian needlework patterns are also available in our Victorian Embroidery Pattern Package, at *victorianvoices.net/clipart/misc/embroidery.shtml*

Happy stitching!

—Moira Allen, Editor
VictorianVoices.net

Persian Applique Embroidery

CONTINUOUS TABLE-COVER BORDER—ORANGE.

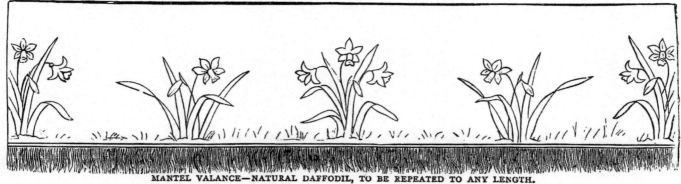

MANTEL VALANCE—NATURAL DAFFODIL, TO BE REPEATED TO ANY LENGTH.

MANTEL VALANCE—CONTINUOUS CONVENTIONAL THISTLE.

MANTEL VALANCE—CONVENTIONAL LILY, TO BE REPEATED TO ANY LENGTH.

MANTEL VALANCE—CONVENTIONAL; REPEAT FESTOONS TO DESIRED LENGTH.

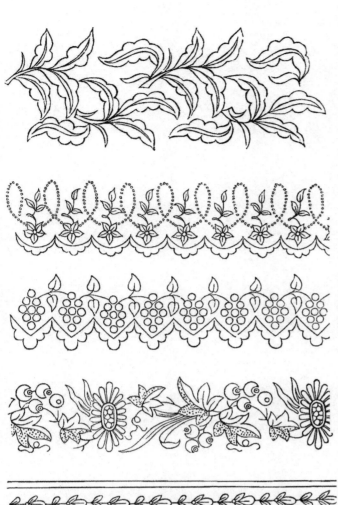

- 43 -

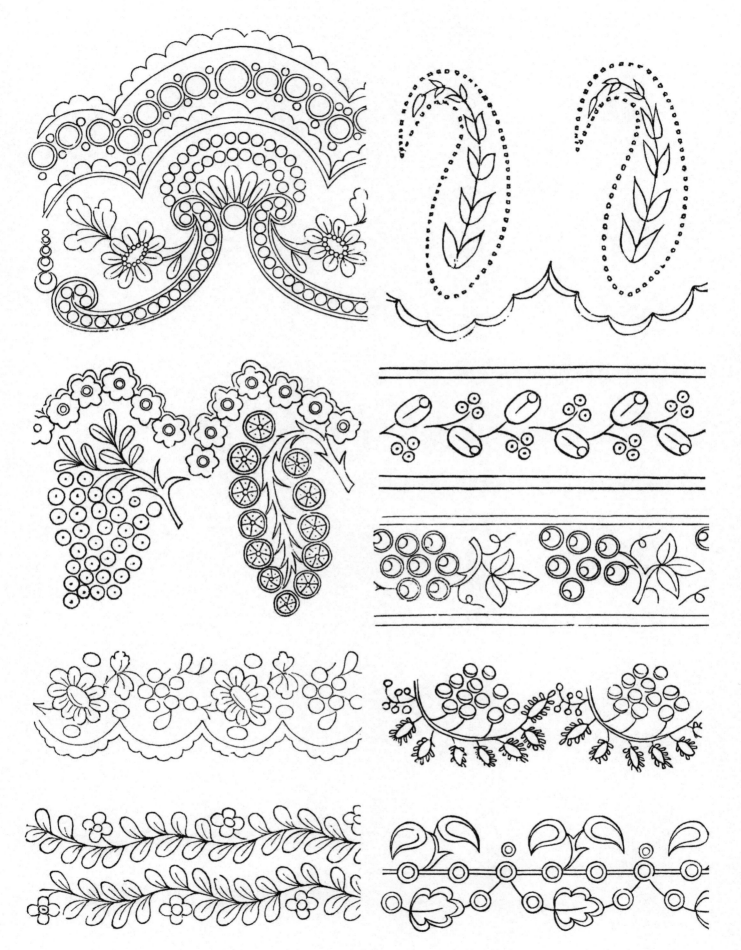

BRYONY.

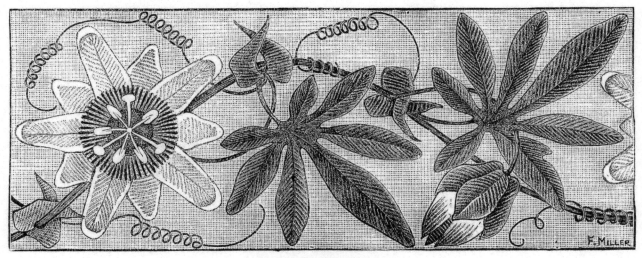

PASSION FLOWER BORDER.

WILD CLEMATIS.

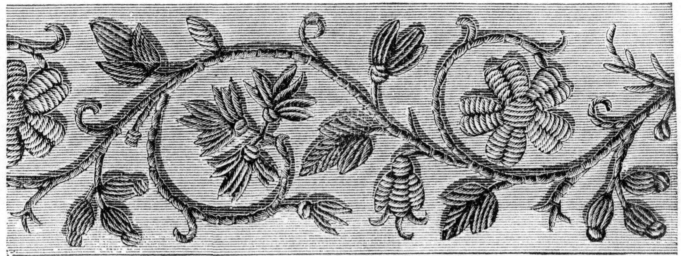

Dresden lace on a cambric ground.

Imitation of Dresden lace on canvas with
openwork ground.

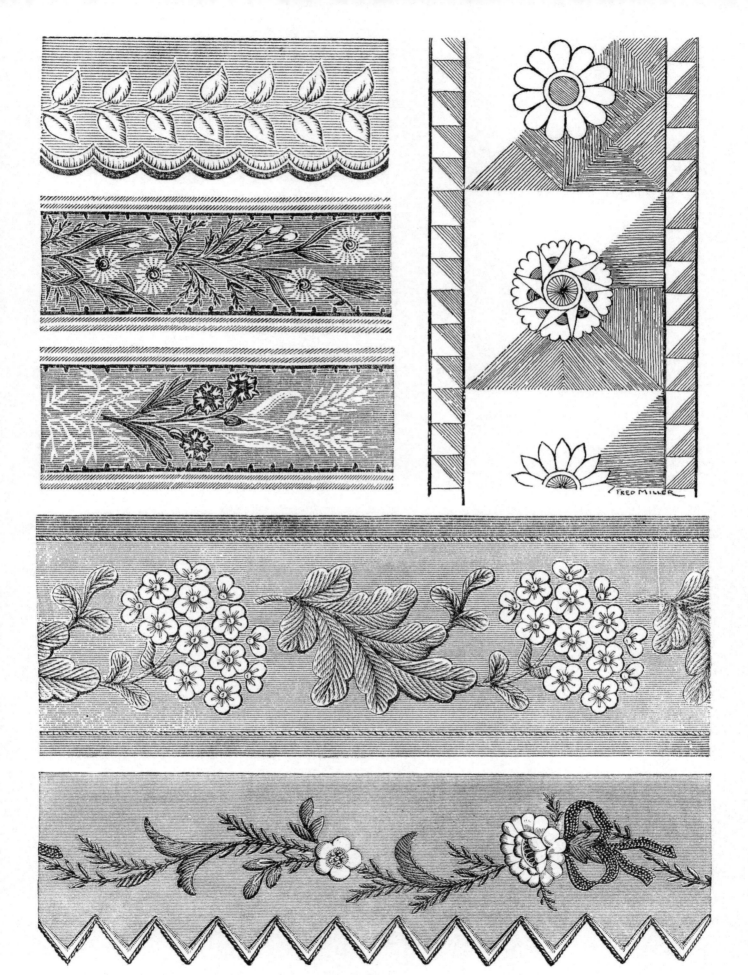

MANTEL-BOARD BORDER.

RICHELIEU EMBROIDERY.

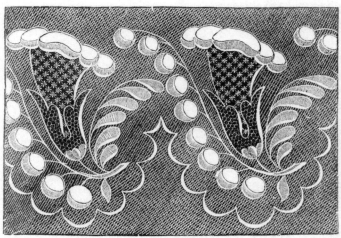

FLOUNCING.

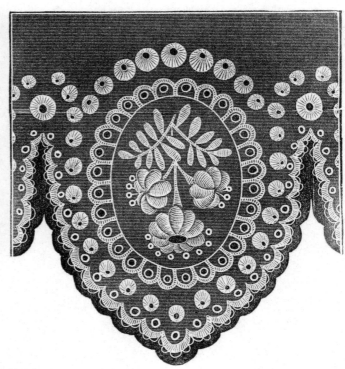

TRIMMING : APPLIQUE.

-71-

SAMPLE DRAWN UP.

SAMPLE DRAWN UP.

HONITON LACE.

BRODERIE ANGLAISE FOR A SKIRT.

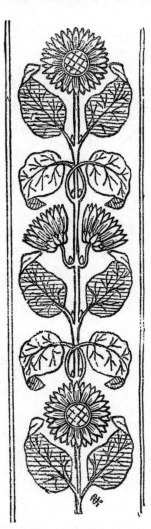

DESIGN FOR SUMMER CURTAIN OR PORTIERE.

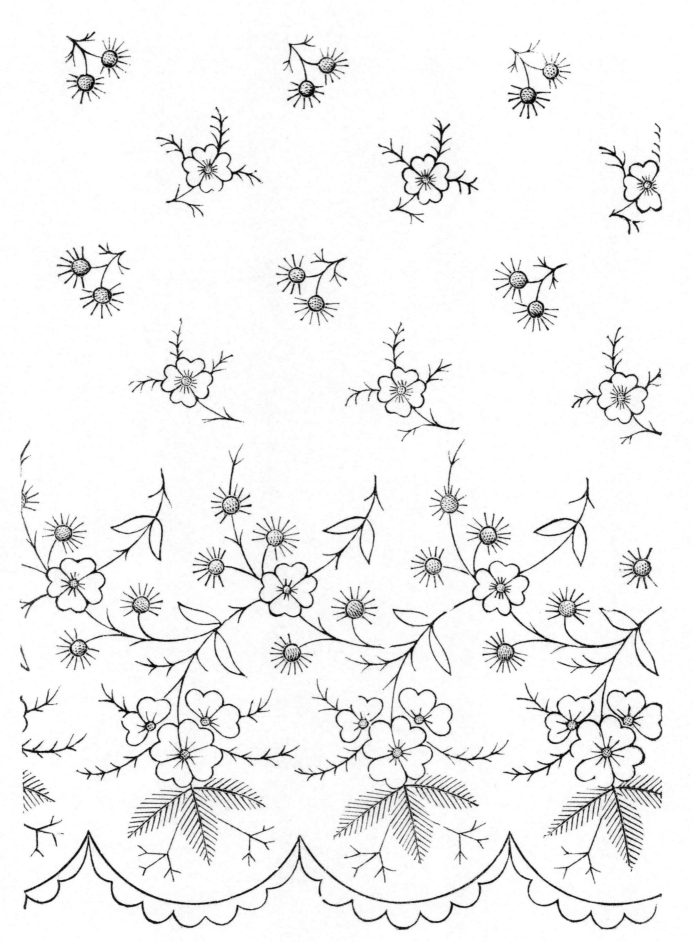

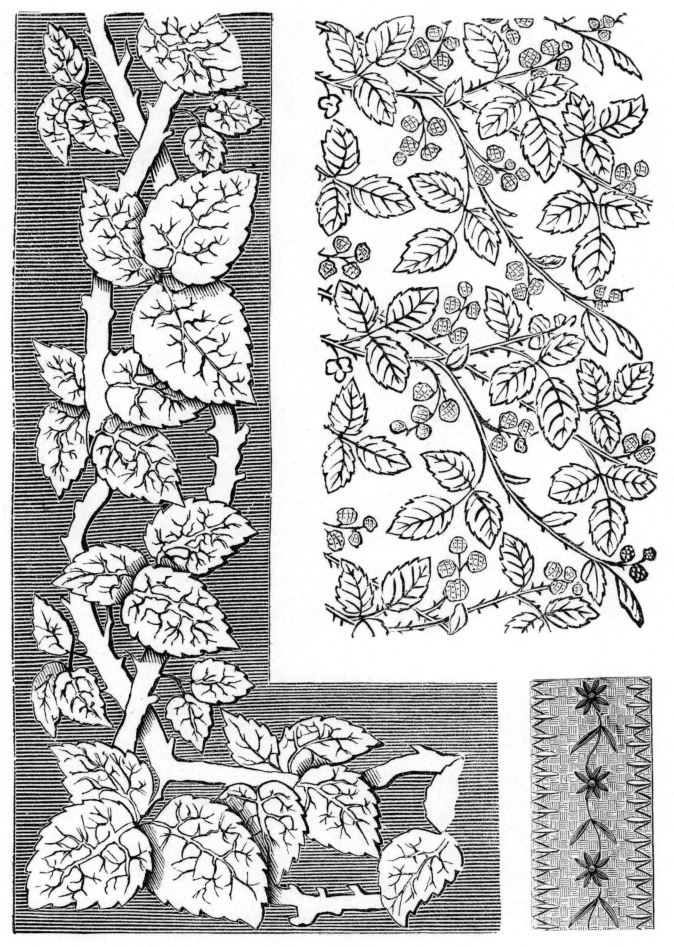

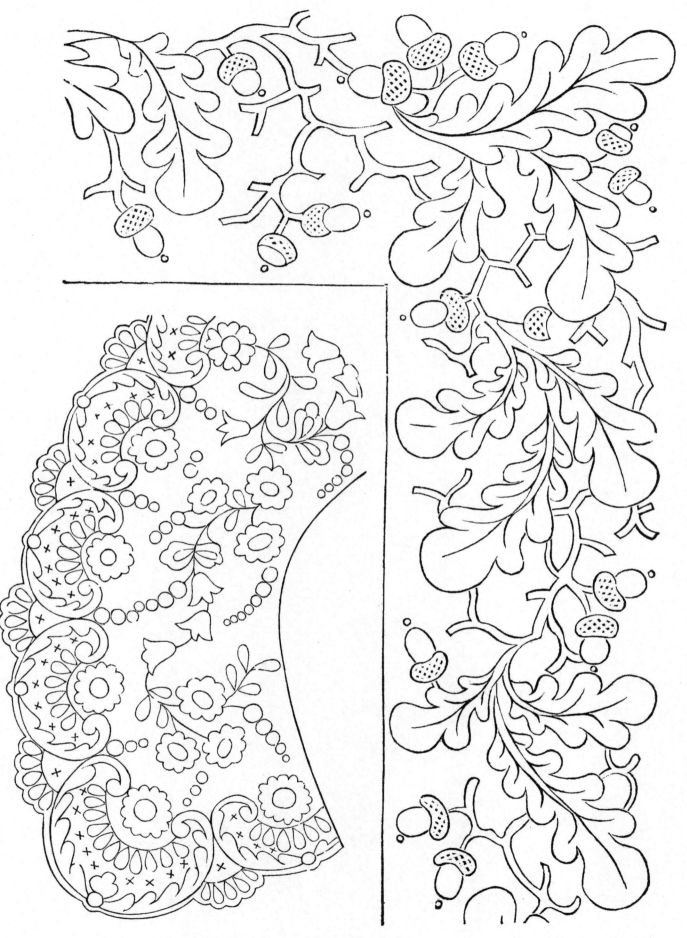

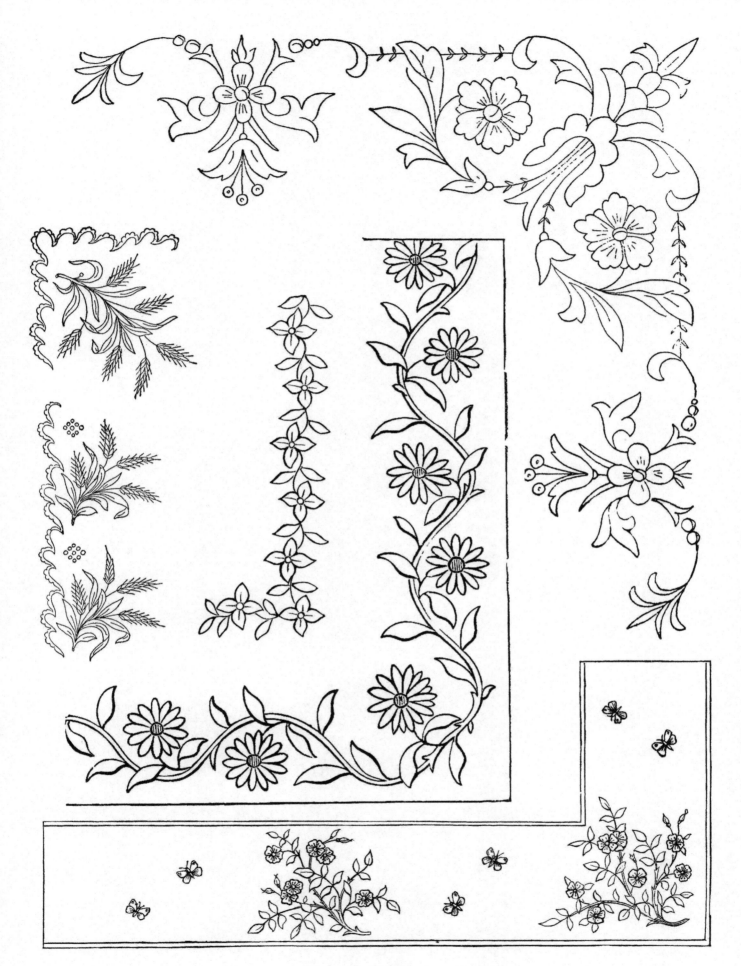

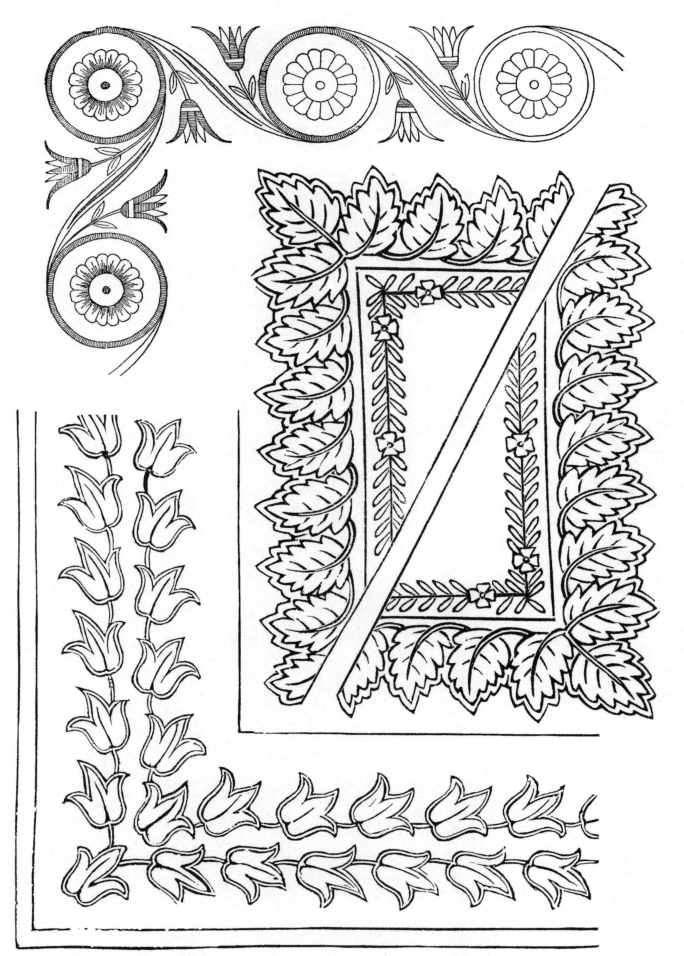

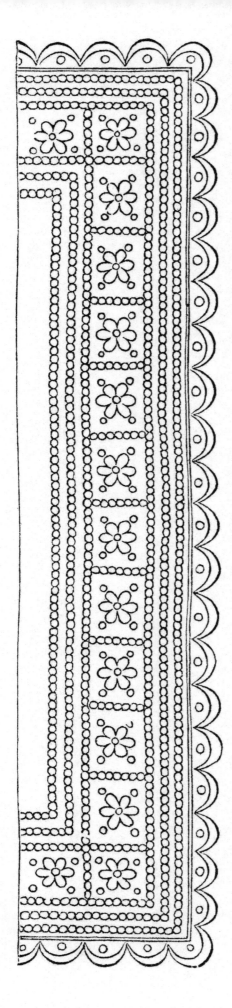

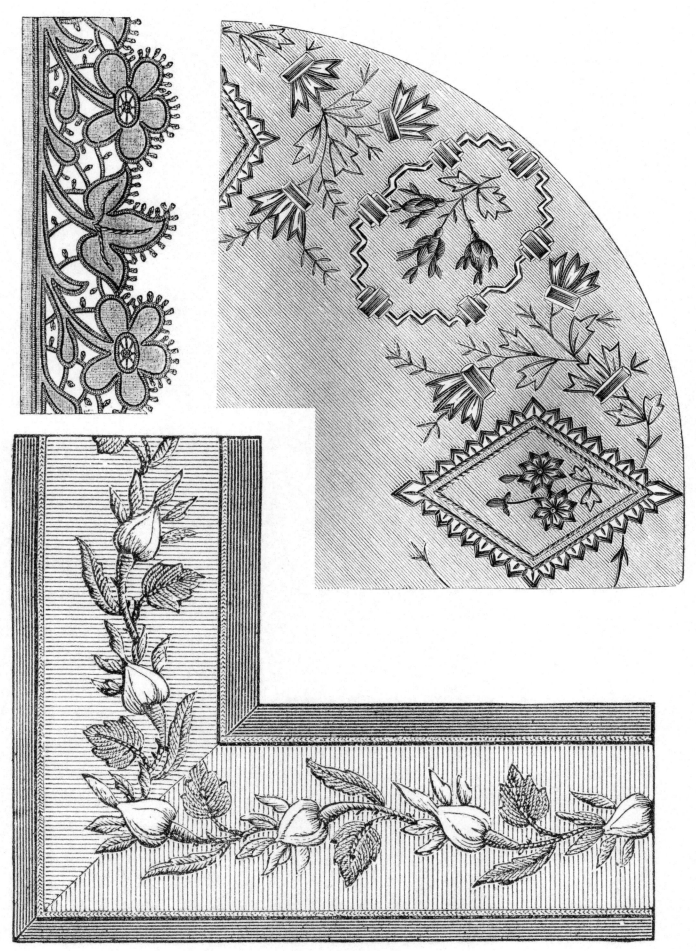

VELVET AND PLUSH LAMBREQUIN.

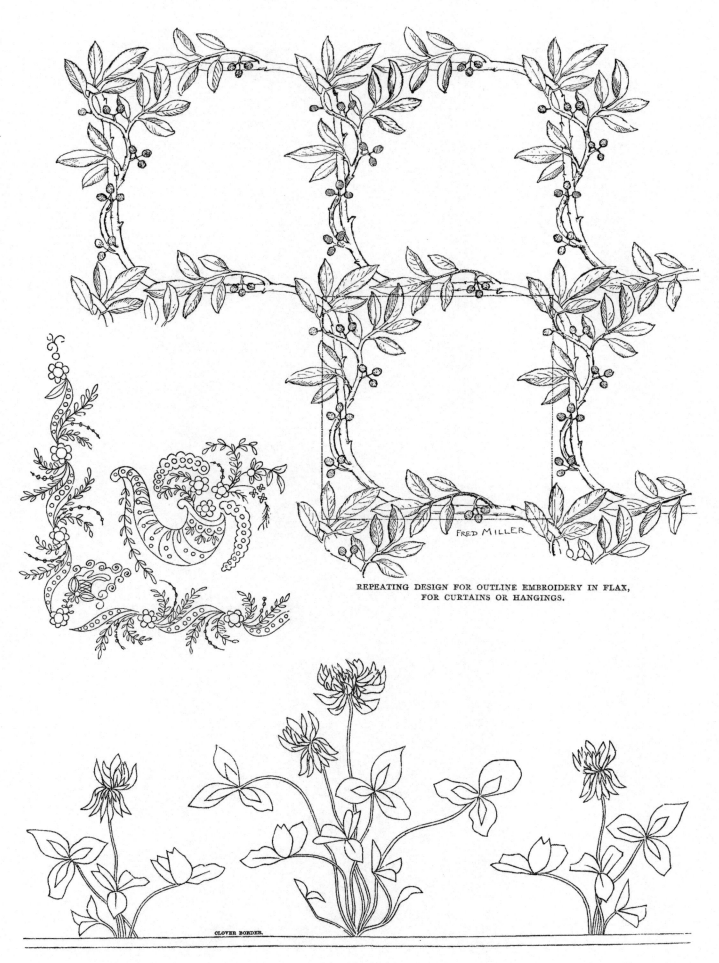

FRED MILLER

REPEATING DESIGN FOR OUTLINE EMBROIDERY IN FLAX,
FOR CURTAINS OR HANGINGS.

CLOVER BORDER.

APPLIQUE BORDER

SLIPPER IN EMBROIDERY.

- 131 -

Thank you for your purchase! I hope you have enjoyed these beautiful Victorian floral and botanical border patterns. Your purchase of this book also entitles you to download these patterns electronically at *tinyurl.com/FloralBorders*. If you have any difficulties with your download, please contact editors@victorianvoices.net for assistance.

Printed in Great Britain
by Amazon

22683631R00077